DOWNSIZING INTUITIVELY

My journey and tips in
selling the family home
to secure my future

RUBY ROBINSON

Copyright © 2023 Ruby Robinson.

All rights reserved. No part of this book may be reproduced, stored, or transmitted by any means—whether auditory, graphic, mechanical, or electronic—without written permission of both publisher and author, except in the case of brief excerpts used in critical articles and reviews. Unauthorized reproduction of any part of this work is illegal and is punishable by law.

*To my mother for her inspiration and guidance,
and my husband for his limitless support.*

CONTENTS

Chapter 1	The Arrival	1
Chapter 2	Should I Stay Or Should I Go?	7
Chapter 3	Taking Stock	15
Chapter 4	My Compass	23
Chapter 5	Weekend Away - A Leap of Faith in Intuition	33
Chapter 6	Developing Intuition	43
Chapter 7	Reflection and Decision	51
Chapter 8	How to Tell the Children	61
Chapter 9	Putting the House on the Market	67
Chapter 10	Waiting For The Hammer To Fall	79
Chapter 11	Navigating the Emotional Terrain of Downsizing	83
Chapter 12	Transitions and Connections - Saying Goodbye to a Beloved Community	91
Chapter 13	Moving Day: Embracing a New Beginning	97
Chapter 14	Embracing Transformation with Courage, Intuition and Humour	105

CHAPTER 1

THE ARRIVAL

"Life is a series of natural and spontaneous changes. Don't resist them - that only creates sorrow. Let reality be reality. Let things flow naturally forward in whatever way they like."

— Lao Tzu

We were not far away from Charlotte's house. The drive had been long distance-wise, around 11 hours, but we'd been energised with the excitement of moving interstate and time had passed quickly. In minutes we would arrive. There were many questions before us but no doubts. My intuition had brought us here and my intuition had so far served me well.

The sun had already disappeared beyond the horizon

and vivid hues of deep pink, purple, and some orange filled the sky. I took it as a good omen for a rich and colourful life to come.

My husband, Matt, tapped me lightly on the shoulder, "What are you thinking about honey?"

He continued with a voice of concern, "Are you okay?" I turned and smiled reassuringly. "Everything's wonderful", I said softly, "I know in my heart this is the right thing to do but I also know that part of starting over involves letting some things go and I am still coming to grips with that. It may take a while."

A man who was typically full of conversation and questions, Matt nodded silently. He believed in my intuition and backed me unreservedly. He would also have known what I was going through.

The moment was interrupted by movement on the back seat. Our two Cavoodles, perhaps also sensing we were to arrive soon, started wagging their tails excitedly. In addition to regular stops for us, the trip had also been punctuated with breaks for one-year-old Maggie and three-month-old Tilly. Even before we had left, the dogs, especially the older Maggie, had sensed the move was afoot. Still, they had travelled well and seemed happy just to be with us wherever that was going to be.

We had sold our family home near Kiama, south of Sydney, after having decided to move interstate to the Sunshine Coast in Queensland where Charlotte, one of my daughters, lived with Alex, her fiancé. Matt and I had been running a modest videography business that had been hit hard during COVID so the idea of moving to a fresh market had also been appealing. Previously, I'd been a psychologist but hadn't been practicing for several years and had turned my skills to asking the questions for the video interviews and doing the admin and books. It wasn't my sort of work, but it had helped pay the bills.

It was hard to believe that after all the hours, days and weeks of preparation; the stress associated with the selling of the family home; the saying goodbye; and the actual moving; we were finally about to arrive. We had been thankful that during the trip, family and close friends had helped fill the hours with phone calls. Knowing how long and tiring the drive was going to be, they kept calling us with concern for our welfare and support for our decision. Each of them knew we were taking a gigantic step and one that would fill us with all sorts of emotions—from excitement and adventure to the grief of saying farewell to our children and our wonderfully supportive community. It was so nice to hear their voices on that long journey. We knew we were loved.

We turned into Charlotte's street. Funny that it was just months before that we had been here and the 'epiphany' of moving came about.

We'd been up to visit on a whim during the last weekend in January and had been having a lovely time. It was

Alex who had casually broached the idea of us moving here as he knew we had been thinking of downsizing though we had never considered the Sunshine Coast. It was a Eureka moment for me and I turned to Matt with excitement in my eyes, a look he had seen before.

Of course, the decision was not made there. There were many things to consider over the course of several months, but I knew in my heart from the outset that the move would work. Apart from Charlotte and Alex, we each had a connection on the Sunshine Coast and that also encouraged us. My oldest girlfriend, Sally, whom I'd known since I was five, lived not far from Charlotte. And Matt also had a life-long friend living in the region. When we first told each of them months before that we were seriously considering moving up, they were overjoyed and welcoming. Luckily, Matt's old friend and his wife had a granny flat they were offering us while they were overseas and it would be ready for us shortly. In the meantime, Charlotte's home would be our home. For us, it was another sign that my intuition was sound. Such a courageous move by so many standards was an opportunity to downsize, liberate some capital for our eventual retirement and have a fresh start. I was inspired by the words of Eleanor Roosevelt when she said that *"Courage is more exhilarating than fear and in the long run it is easier. We do not have to become heroes overnight. Just one step at a time, meeting each thing that comes up, seeing it is not as dreadful as it appeared, discovering we have the strength to stare it down."*

There it was—Charlotte's driveway! We were arriving! The memories of the last weeks flashed in my mind like a movie: the house being sold; the last-minute packing; our furniture and belongings on their way into storage; the tears goodbye; and the drive up.

Before the car came to a halt, there was Charlotte bounding out of her front door to greet us. My tears ran freely as she excitedly ran squealing and jumping into my arms. "I can't believe you're here!" she cried, "you did it!" It was such a beautiful welcome.

The hardest part had been done. We had arrived. Now all we had to do was find a house to call our own and establish our lives again. I knew my intuition was going to be needed again.

CHAPTER 2

SHOULD I STAY OR SHOULD I GO?

"Often when you think you're at the end of something, you're at the beginning of something else."

–Fred Rogers

I'm fairly uncomplicated! I don't pay too much attention to detail and am more of a 'fly-by-the-seat-of-my-pants' kind of woman. Since my divorce, I'd decided to live my life more freely, have fun with my kids and then, when Matt came along, share it all with him. Matt and I had worked for ourselves in different businesses over the years: me as a herbalist and then with my psychology practise; and Matt as a radio journalist, running a communication/

marketing business and, finally, running a videography business with me after I had finished my practise. The funny thing was that while we had always had business goals and KPIs, the thought of possible retirement and what was to come after that had not featured in our minds. That all changed when Matt and I spent a weekend with Abby in October 2021.

I first met Abby at uni when I was doing my psychology post-grad. There I was at forty as a mature-age student sitting in the computer lab feeling quite old compared with all these young, fit-looking students when there before me was another mature age student just like me. Once we started chatting, I discovered we had a lot more in common than our age and a love for psychology—we had similar life experiences. It was uncanny!

I should explain that way back then, not many people had desktop computers at home and laptops were a pretty new and expensive thing to have. So, gaining access in the computer lab was ultra-important. Abby and I would arrive early with our lunches, thermoses and plenty of water to ensure we didn't need to leave the desk once we commanded possession. And we would talk and laugh and laugh and talk some more. Strangely enough, we got our work done as well.

That was around 17 years ago and we've been close friends ever since. As you can imagine, during that time, many things had changed in our lives so there were always things to catch up about. Abby had continued developing her psychology practise and had become very successful. Occasionally she'd call to sound out an issue and pick my brains and I would do likewise but, mainly, our catch ups were all about us and our families: our growing children and their respective relationships; our aging parents including those who had passed away; and, of course, our relationships.

Apart from these regular phone chats, we also set time to catch up in person a couple of times a year, usually over a weekend. Abby is a self-confessed, passionate 'foodie' and a wonderful cook so, when at her place, we'd always have a beautiful home-cooked meal and delicious wines. That particular weekend in October was no different except for the eye-opening conversation that was to change our lives.

After the initial chit-chat over the mandatory bottle of bubbles, we sat down in anticipation for the meal (Abby always liked to present the food to us sitting as if in a restaurant). While waiting to be awed by what was to be placed on the table, I remember glancing outside to appreciate the view. We were up quite high and looked out over the water. The light was draining from the horizon, paving the way for a pinkish-reddish sky. I remembered the old saying about 'red sky at night, sailors delight' and felt it was an appropriate reflection of the beautiful atmosphere we were all sharing inside the home. It was certainly a comforting and reassuring feeling.

Abby sat the plate of glistening roast lamb and veggies in the middle of the table. The wonderful odour made me salivate and I knew she had outdone herself. We toasted to good health with the aged Shiraz we had offered and started to eat. There was a moment of silence as we started on our first mouthfuls and then Abby looked at Matt and I and asked, "So, what's your plan for leaving the workforce, guys?"

I swallowed the tender morsel I was savouring and smiled. "Oh, you know me, I don't have a specific plan yet but it's funny you ask because for the last year I've had the feeling that we need to prepare the house for sale!" Then, turning to include Matt, I added, "So, over the last year we've landscaped the backyard with a lovely firepit, we've paved the side passage, replaced the weathered western wall and…" I said proudly with the hint of a pause, "I painted the house!"

Matt wiped his mouth with a napkin and smiled, "Yep, she did a fantastic job and the painting alone improved the value of the house, not to mention the lovely backyard we have now." Then, leaning back in his chair, he continued in his relaxed manner, "and while we didn't have a plan or time period to sell, Ruby just felt we needed to put the effort, time and money into the house and, as I trust her intuition, I happily went along. As to an exit plan," he continued, "no, we don't have one."

Abby nodded her understanding while topping up all

our glasses and then explained, "I've been chatting to friends and asking about their retirement plans and the biggest challenge everyone seems to face is…" she paused and looked at each of us with her big smile and then continued, "how to manage a comfortable lifestyle while no longer actively generating an income."

Abby then told us how she had mapped out the coming years with what she called her 'exit plan'. It involved selling her home, investing in another less expensive house or apartment and then using some of her inheritance to buy another and turn it into an Airbnb. She had it all mapped out.

"Wow!" I said surprisingly, "you've really been thinking this through but you're quite a few years away from retirement age as we're the same age."

"Yes, we are," she replied, "but I didn't want to leave it until then, it's too important!"

I looked at Matt, "This is a bit of a wake-up call," I said seriously, "I've had the feeling we needed to work on the house and maybe sell but in terms of a concrete plan, I've not given it much thought."

As the dinner and discussion progressed (and more wine consumed), I realised that Abby was right and that Matt and I were both getting to an age where we needed to be planning ahead. Apart from my car, a set of golf clubs and a kayak, the bulk of my assets was in the family home. Moreover, Matt and I had little superannuation set aside. Despite so many similarities to our lovely host, my situation was so different.

We left that weekend full of important questions, the main one being, how could we ever leave the workforce and sustain a comfortable future for the next forty-something years.

And so, in order to find some answers, we continued discussing the same question between us and also involved some of our friends. We came to realise that many of them were also coming to terms with the issues of potentially running out of money, of coping with inflation, rising health care costs (both of us having some health issues), real estate market fluctuations and the almost taboo subject of the untimely death of a spouse. There was so much to consider. Some of our friends, like Abby, were well advanced in their planning and had already sought the advice from financial planners while others, like us, were just coming to terms with the issues and were a long way off from finding answers. What was clear was that our journey had begun.

TAKEAWAY

- What did you glean from this conversation?
- Can you identify with a similar problem in your life or perhaps someone you know?

- Do you have an exit plan? Do you need to start thinking about these sorts of issues?
- Are there any potential health factors that may need you or your partner being hospitalised (e.g., knee or hip replacement) as medical issues can hamper your ability to provide an income and the costs can be high.

CHAPTER 3

TAKING STOCK

"We need to regularly stop and take stock; to sit down and determine within ourselves which things are worth valuing and which things are not; which risks are worth the cost and which are not? Even the most confusing or hurtful aspects of life can be made more tolerable by clear seeing and by choice."

—Epictetus

While Abby had a well-defined plan to exit the workforce, Matt and I were uncertain about how we would manage without working. We chatted about this on the way back from Abby's and I realised I needed to give it a lot more thought. Our house was already recently painted and partly renovated so, in many ways, I thought it was ready to sell. But I knew that was the most obvious factor to consider and others—our work, friends and being part of the local community— also needed to be thought about before making any decisions. The most crucial concerns, however, were working out the logistics of how to downsize the family home and the emotional impact it could have on our children. The latter weighed heavily on me.

During that time, my eldest son, Jackson, his partner, Anna, and my youngest son, Harley, lived with us while attending university. The arrangement was financially beneficial for them as they could save money by avoiding paying rent elsewhere. They had part-time jobs which helped them pay some board, but they still relied on us for support. Our exit plan, therefore, would have a significant impact on them. If we decided to downsize and move to a different region, they'd have to search for a rental property that was affordable and suitable for their needs. As uni students, they didn't have substantial savings and depended on us. So, I was uncertain whether downsizing was the right decision for us to make at that time.

Days after 'the' conversation with Abby, I casually mentioned her suggestion to Jackson. "Abby raised the topic of leaving work," I started, "and I think she made a good point. We should start considering our retirement plan. We've been thinking about downsizing and selling the house in two years."

Jackson looked at me with sincerity and innocence and asked, "Why wait two years, Mum? Why not do it now?"

His concern warmed my heart. Holding back tears I replied, "You and Harley still have two more years of university and are living at home. That's why we're waiting." Jackson reassured me, "Don't worry about us, Mum. We'll be fine."

As I heard the tone of his voice, I felt a shiver run down my spine. Until that moment, the thought of selling the family home had been on the back burner. With that conversation, however, I felt I was given permission to act on the plan sooner than later. This talk took place approximately six months before I realised we were going to move interstate to the Sunshine Coast.

After that chat, I began to explore different solutions to our situation. I realised that one was to sell the house and downsize to free up some capital. This meant exploring the housing market to find something nearby which was affordable which, in turn, meant continuing to prepare the house for an eventual sale. Another solution was to continue working and expanding our current business and income and stay put for the time being and wait for an opportunity to present itself.

By this stage in my life, I'd developed a high level of faith in my intuition. That led me to believe that the correct solution would present itself, even if I didn't know what that would look like. So, together with Matt, we began our search for another house. Firstly, we evaluated the housing market to determine whether downsizing was viable. We also needed to find a suitable home that would fit our budget and meet our needs.

Furthermore, I realised that if we were to sell our current home, we'd need to assess its selling points to determine how much money to spend on preparing it for sale. After careful consideration, while we knew that the kitchen and bathroom required renovations, we realised they were not justifiable expenses. In the end, we decided to invest in improving the front garden and refurbishing the interior by removing the old, shabby looking carpet and sanding the beautiful Kauri Pine floorboards. This would also give us an opportunity to purchase furniture that would better showcase the house for sale and serve as a valuable asset for our future home.

Selling the family home, however, presented two challenges: practical matters and assessing our emotional well-being. Being a Cancerian, my home held great significance. It symbolized family and nurturing, and I cherished the memories of having raised my children in my home. Like any loving mother, I always prioritized their needs over mine. At each step of my life, I'd considered what they needed before I could even consider what I needed. So, letting go of all that was challenging and, from an emotional standpoint, made the decision more difficult. I had to change that value of selflessness and remind myself that taking care of my needs was okay. That was not easy. Afterall, this was their home as well.

As a psychologist, I understand that the thought of selling had placed a massive burden of guilt on me. My eldest daughter, Emma, was not thrilled when she heard we planned to sell the family home and shared her grief with me. Even though she no longer lived there, Emma told me that the house gave her a connection to her family and the community in which she'd grown up. Selling it meant a loss for her. It also meant she couldn't physically pop in to visit me whenever she liked. Her anguish made me briefly pause and wonder if I was doing the right thing. Thankfully, by this stage, I'd learnt to hear and trust my inner voice and knew it would never lead me astray. All I had to do was to follow.

Emma was not the only child affected by this move. My youngest, Harley, had never left the home or lived away from me. Unlike the bond I had with my other children, ours was unique. There was a great sense of harmony between us, and that made it easy for us to live together. This decision to downsize challenged that connection. I had this painful longing to hold on to my youngest one as long as I could. But, at the same time, I had an inkling that it was time to cut the cord and let him 'fly the coop'.

My conversation with Jackson was a turning point. I'd been holding off making a decision, but his words gave me the confidence to act. It lifted the burden from my shoulders and was a relief to know that my children were adults and completely capable of being on their own. I no longer felt guilty about selling the family home and focusing on my needs. My guilt had been addressed. I also learnt that communication is paramount in any relationship. Having an open, mature conversation with my adult child about our financial plans and ideas opened up a window for a solution. Jackson may have been caught off guard that day, but I had started the frank conversation and taken into account his thoughts and feelings about selling the house. I'd not hidden it from him and that gave me great relief.

That day, my goal of raising my children to become functioning, contributing and productive members of society was realized. There was no need for me to carry unnecessary responsibility for my adult children. I realised it's okay to sell the family home and not hold the guilt. Selling the family home didn't mean closing the door on them; the children could always visit or return to our new home.

By now, we had taken into account the possible impact on each of the family members. But as I started to process in my mind all the implications of selling our home, there was one I had missed: I realized that when Matt and I had met, he'd moved into my family's home; we had never established a home together. Downsizing, I realised, would give us an opportunity to do just that. So, as a couple, Matt and I were moving into new territory, and that was a significant step. Needless to say, I was looking forward to starting this chapter in our lives.

TAKEAWAY

- Can you identify with this situation? Are you carrying too much responsibility? Do you carry the burden of guilt when it comes to your children? If so, I suggest you have a calm, adult conversation with them. Outline your thoughts, ideas and plans for 'your' future. It might come as a surprise to your children, but at least you have started a conversation and given them time to process the concept.
- Make a list of pros and cons for your home to determine what could be improved for sale purposes and what should be left for the prospective owner.
- Get a market appraisal for your house.
- Search online to see what's on the market in the area you're drawn to.
- Check the equity in your home. Considering agent fees and stamp duty, how much capital would you free up with a sale? How much would you need for retirement?

CHAPTER 4

MY COMPASS

"I think of how life takes unexpected twists and turns, sometimes through sheer happenstance, sometimes through calculated decisions. In the end, it can all be called fate, but to me, it is more a matter of faith."

—Emily Giffin

Although our business had been steady before COVID, it slowed down to a trickle during and after the pandemic. We realised it would not match our plans. Downsizing seemed the best option to free up assets, put them into a super fund and make the most of our finances. A substantial super balance meant we could draw on this fund as an income when we stopped working—at least that was the plan! This made me more confident that we were on the right path, but I didn't want to rely solely on that. We had read up on retirement planning and discussed these ideas loosely with friends of similar age and situations over the years, so we were feeling more prepared for this stage of our lives. I knew, however, that it was time to walk the talk! It was time for action!

I soon came to realise that downsizing can be a daunting task with lots of twists and turns. Factors like emotional attachment to friends and the community; decision fatigue from sorting through a lifetime of possessions; the pure physical exertion of packing, cleaning and sorting; the complicated and stressful financial process of selling and buying a home; and the fear of the unknown—can all individually and collectively make it a challenging process. On the other hand, and most importantly, downsizing can be a smart financial move when done correctly. It can open opportunities for a better and more secure lifestyle which is why we had set out on this journey.

With all these challenges and important decisions before us, we wanted to ensure we were heading in the right direction. And to provide us with that assurance, we decided to seek the advice of a financial planner to help us navigate the process. I had a good one in mind and knew he would steer us in the right direction. My father had been doing business with Bob for a long time and we'd had less important dealings with him over the years. This time, it was going to be a different conversation with much more money to invest. Again, I trusted my intuition.

As it turned out, Bob played an essential role in helping us with our decision-making process. He made us aware, for example, that there were many aspects we needed to consider. The most essential was coming up with an actual plan for our retirement. In the subsequent discussions, we also had to consider the real estate market's volatility and check the value of our current home. Luckily, while our house was in a reasonably well sought after location and we had seen some nearby houses go for a lot more than what we had thought, we weren't sure about the dynamic nature of the market. Prices had been increasing and no one was sure when and if the bubble was going to burst. It seemed timing was critical.

With this in mind, Bob set about mapping various scenarios and guided us through the available options. This was great as it gave us a clearer insight into setting a budget depending on how the real estate market could react and what we could get for our house.

All this was well and good, but I was starting to realise first-hand how much of a huge decision downsizing can be, not to mention how complicated it can get. Making such life-changing decisions is bound to cause stress, and, in my case, it was significant. I'd lived in this family home for fifteen years and in the same community for thirty!

Leaving behind all those memories, friends and community connections was not going to be easy.

Apart from the strong emotional connection to the house, our friends and the lovely street in which we lived, I also had to deal with all our belongings. I'd purchased the house following my divorce and had lived comfortably with my half of the split. A relatively small house, it had been ideal for my needs through those subsequent years. But then Matt had moved in ten years ago bringing a lot of his 'stuff'! Essentially, we had two households crammed into one small house. Of course, we rationalised much of what we had but Matt liked to hang onto 'treasured' items or those he thought would be useful at some later date (the tool shed, for example, was full of bits and pieces and don't let me start on what he had stored under the house). Downsizing would mean sorting through our belongings and 'stuff', a chore we would have to deal with.

But that was for later. First, one of the biggest questions we asked ourselves was where we were going to move. We sat down one afternoon with a chilled bottle of wine and started to brainstorm. We knew we wanted to live on the coast with possible water views so that we could see the moon on the water (very romantic but something we had always wanted). We also wanted to be near family yet not too far from an airport. Ideally, the location would also have a north-facing aspect. We wanted proximity to community amenities and transportation and the house needed to be large enough to accommodate visiting family but not too large so that we could manage the maintenance. Access to an ocean, community swimming pool or a pool on the property would also be a bonus. And, of course, it also had to fit within our budget. Easy!

The last time I'd gone through this type of exercise I was newly single, had four children and a new job. I'd talked to a friend about manifesting after having attended a workshop/seminar and then reading more about asking for what I wanted. She guided me to take the time to practice 'vibrating'—an energy pattern generated within the self, and, in this case, at a level of appreciation—and then ask very clearly and specifically, for what I desired. Armed with a new process, I also wrote down five or six points about the new house I was looking to buy. Each morning on my regular walk, I'd focus on the things I appreciated in my life. This aligned me with my inner being. Following this, I'd then repeat several times, out loud, the things I'd listed. Continuing this pattern morning and night for the next few weeks, my future home presented itself, exactly as I had manifested, down to the exact amount I was prepared to pay.

Back to the new search, I started exploring different areas, looking a little further away from where we were, to find something more affordable. "How far is too far?" we wondered. We considered further down the NSW South Coast (e.g., Jervis Bay, Mollymook), where we thought prices would be more reasonable. Didn't we get a surprise? We soon discovered that prices had skyrocketed due to COVID and the ability for people to work remotely from regional areas. Many had taken the opportunity for a 'sea change', creating greater wellbeing in their lives.

Moving further south would also mean being even further from our two kids living in Sydney and from the airport, and thus access to Charlotte in Queensland. Seeing the inflated prices down south, it dawned on us that we may not have been the only ones who'd made the decision to downsize and we may have missed the boat. Nevertheless, we persisted with our search.

Thanks to the advice from Bob, we set about having our house valued by Steve, a trusted real estate agent. He explained the current situation with the market and while he joked about not having a crystal ball; he at least gave us a ballpark range of what we could expect if we were to list our property straight away as well as if we waited some months. His recommendation was to sell sooner rather than later before the unrealistic prices tumbled. Again, my intuition told me now was the best time.

With this information, Bob set a budget for our financial future. This allowed us to calculate how much would remain towards a property. Basically, we tried to balance our desire for comfortable living with our need to maintain a certain level of financial security. We weighed the benefits and drawbacks of different housing options, including a duplex, townhouse, or smaller house. Sometimes, we simply discussed ideas as we went, while other times, we made a list of pros and cons to help clarify the decision-making process.

I discovered that finding a house that matched our requirements was easier said than done. Our experience with searching had its challenges. My initial searches were either online or within our existing locale and I set about doing house inspections. I must say that each time I visited somewhere, I felt disappointed in terms of quality and price. Was what I was looking for out of our price bracket? Were we dreaming? Perhaps the right place had not yet hit the market. My previous property searching had led me to believe the right property would present itself at the right time. I just needed to be patient and let my intuition guide me. But still, the challenge was to find a property that would meet our criteria. Weeks went by. Nothing presented itself! Interestingly, I didn't use the 'manifesting approach' during this time. Perhaps I knew intuitively that this was not the right time or place? It seemed we had stalled and, for a while, I felt deflated. I knew deep down, however, that something was out there for us. But where was it?

We knew that we could also look at an even smaller house than our existing or an apartment as the kids weren't going to be living with us. Those options would be less expensive and low maintenance, but I didn't feel ready for apartment living and, besides, we needed to have at least a spare bedroom or two for when family (including eventual grandchildren) and friends would visit. Plus, we had two dogs! Matt and I considered them as 'our children' and, as part of our family, their needs had to be accommodated in the decision-making process.

That led us to discussions about the options for a duplex or a townhouse. We looked at one duplex and it had a small yard and then realised that most duplexes are built to maximise the land area at the sacrifice of the yard—not good for the dogs—and the townhouses we saw were pretty much the same as a duplex but came with a strata title which we didn't want.

We also discovered in our research that downsizing could take different paths. Some people prefer the open road and a comfortable RV for years while deciding where to live. Others choose to take up residence on a cruise ship, sailing the world in comfort, all meals prepared, no cleaning to worry about and always meeting people and hearing wonderful stories. Perhaps that could be something for us in the future when we no longer had pets or young grandchildren, but it certainly wasn't an option for us until then.

What was clear for us through this early stage of downsizing, was that the process itself can be fraught with challenges—twists and turns that are not as simple as you might first think. You absolutely need a clear vision and a plan, for it is a journey! Yes, we got some great advice from our financial planner, the real estate agent and our friends, but what I realised was that my intuition was like my personal compass helping guide me along the way. It was that which reassured me.

TAKEAWAY

If you have identified your need to downsize, here are factors to consider. Make a list for each factor or tick it off when done:

1. Have a chat with your financial planner and or accountant.
2. Get a current market appraisal for your property.
3. What sort of property are you looking for? What is your 'wish list'?
4. Which locations do you need to consider?
5. Get a clear idea of the costs of buying and selling (fees, stamp duty etc).
6. List your emotional connections to the community and the friends you have including your involvement in sports, hobbies, clubs and social activities.
7. Look for those connections in the areas you are looking at moving. (e.g., a golf or tennis or bowls club)

8. Don't wait to downsize 'stuff'. Make a list of your 'stuff' and start getting rid of excesses so when the time comes, you will be ready.
9. Pay attention to your intuition. Do the people you are consulting 'feel' right?

CHAPTER 5

WEEKEND AWAY – A LEAP OF FAITH IN INTUITION

"The more you trust your intuition, the more empowered you become, the stronger you become, and the happier you become."

—Gisele Bundchen

It was the last weekend of January 2022 when I visited Charlotte and her fiancé, Alex, on the Sunshine Coast. One of those 'spur of the moment' decisions, I went there with little expectation or a plan apart from wanting to spend time with Charlotte. It was also a lovely opportunity to catch up with my life-long school friend, Sally, who lived nearby. Little did I know that this impromptu weekend would have such an important effect on my life.

Sunday morning arrived and we'd been having a great time together. Matt and I had commented on how nice the region was with its beaches that allowed us to swim nearly every day. Charlotte and Alex had been scouting for homes to purchase, so naturally, there had been plenty of conversations about real estate and costs. We'd just returned from a morning swim and were chatting over coffee when Alex stunned us with an innocent question.

"Ruby, have you ever considered moving up here?" Alex queried, raising an eyebrow.

And that was it. There was a brief silence as everyone waited for my answer. "No..." I said hesitantly, "in all honesty, that has never come to mind."

As soon as the words left my mouth, I felt a sensation of energy shoot through my body. It was an undeniable sign of my intuitive self.

I glanced at Matt and smiled. Alex's simple question had opened an avenue of possibility which hadn't crossed my mind before—could we move to another state? This would mean much more than merely shifting suburbs. This would be an entire relocation!

"But why not..." I smiled and spun around to face Alex, "why not indeed?"

And right there and then I knew that was exactly what we were going to do. My intuition had taken over and my mind raced with adrenaline.

Matt, knowing the look in my eyes, spoke up cautiously,

"Well, it could be an interesting possibility," he offered carefully, "but there would be a lot to consider and discuss."

I could sense his wrestling with the tiger about to pounce! He knew me too well and could see in my eyes that I had real energy for the idea.

We already had plans for the rest of the day, so decided to change the conversation. My brain, however, was already on the move. The thought of being closer to my daughter stirred something deep within me. There was also the opportunity to be close to Sally, my long-time friend. I couldn't shake those thoughts! Then, not thinking about just myself, I realised this would also give Matt the chance to reconnect with his old friend nearby. On top of that, we'd be able to strengthen our connection with my brother and his wife who had moved to Queensland some thirty years ago. I was bursting with excitement.

Before I knew, it was time for Charlotte to drop us off at the airport and, in the car, my beautiful daughter reopened the conversation.

"Hey Mum," she asked with a mischievous grin, "would you really consider moving up here?

"Well, it could be good," I replied, "and it would be wonderful to live closer to you."

My heart was racing and Matt knew what was on my mind—I wanted to start packing right then and there. I could see, however, that he seemed more hesitant and needed more time to discuss through the practicalities and logic of such a momentous decision.

So, once we were on the plane and buckled in, that's what we did.

"Well…" he started cautiously, "we need to talk about how this would work. You know, plan out what the next steps need to be and all the logistics."

I knew right then that Matt was 'on board' with the notion but was probably trying to catch up with me because he could see that I'd already shifted into gear. He knew that my mind had already gone there.

"If this is the right thing for us to do," he continued, "it means cutting our ties, there are business issues to consider; we'll have to prepare and then list the house for sale…"

I could see his mind churning over the logistics and wrapping his head around what it would all mean. He was already wanting to do the 'man thing' and practically solve the problem. My intuition had already cemented the idea in my mind but I knew it was important to allow Matt the space to process all this as the decision was not mine alone.

The timing of the wine from the flight attendant couldn't have been more perfect. Matt and I agreed we didn't need to be stuck in all the nitty gritty details just yet and, instead, use the time for us both to quietly think about the exciting opportunities that could come our way.

At this time, I remembered something about myself. My rationality and intuition were two distinct things. I had often prided myself on being a 'sensible human' who stuck pretty much to societal norms. But I am human! I didn't arrive at so completely trusting my intuition overnight. My journey had been speckled with decisions that had been made purely on logic or reason alone. One was marrying my first husband, a decision driven by practical considerations and societal expectations. It was also a desperate attempt to hold onto a connection with my mother who had passed a few years prior. In marrying him, I'd silenced the whispers of my intuition and had ignored the subtle warning signs from within.

With time, I learnt the importance of honouring my inner voice and recognized that intuition was not merely a flight of fancy but a profound source of wisdom. I realised that I'd already made some significant life decisions based to a large degree on my intuition: I had chosen to leave that failing marriage; buy my own house; follow my heart to a new partner; and now, here I was considering selling the family home to move interstate. I could see that trusting my intuition had led me down paths of immense personal growth, fulfillment and happiness. Intuition, to me, was not merely an emotional response but a profound knowing. It was a connection to something greater than me: spirit, universal wisdom or intuition; call it what you will!

How liberating and exciting it is just to go where my intuition leads me. There's no pressure to calculate a solution. It's so relaxing letting go of resistant thoughts and allowing the answer to present itself. I don't have to stick with conventional thinking. Imagine if you could let go of the need to justify (even to yourself, never mind others)? The more I thought, the more I liked giving my inner voice a chance to be heard.

The more I thought about it, the deeper it went. The question arose in my mind whether it was important to consider emotions when making significant decisions or to prioritize rational thinking. For me, intuition always served as the initial guide, a subtle nudging, that directed me toward a conclusion. I understood, however, the importance of balancing emotions with rational thinking. While emotions alone could lead to impulsive or hasty decisions, embracing intuition allowed me to tap into deeper wisdom. It was like a delicate dance between my intuition and rationality.

Moving to a new city or state had never been part of my life plan. But the mere thought of living near Charlotte, rekindling our respective friendships with our lifelong friends and reconnecting with my brother and his wife after decades of physical distance, was all appealing. As we had also seen from the weekend's brief foray into the real estate market, the potential financial benefit of moving there seemed a hands-down winner as well.

The days that followed were filled with conversations regarding the logistics of relocating. I also contemplated the potential impact of leaving my existing friends behind and no longer being part of a close community. I realised that, over the years, I'd had many close friends and family members who'd lived far away. I also knew that the geographical distance could impact the nature of relationships. While it was true that I didn't always interact as frequently with friends who lived afar, in most cases, the love and connection remained steadfast. I reasoned that regardless of distance, relationships naturally evolve, but the foundation of true friendship endures.

In the case of my kids, I was certain that distance would have no bearing on our bond. Thanks to technology, I could maintain constant contact with them, bridging the physical gap with a virtual presence and occasional visits. Besides, relocating to the Sunshine Coast with its modern airport would mean we were only ever a short flight away.

I feel it fair to say that when trying to make significant decisions in our lives and where there is an element of risk (whether emotional, financial, reputational, health or well-being), moments of inner conflict can arise. To manage this, I'd found over the years that by embracing patience and allowing the answers to unfold naturally, a deeper sense of clarity would always emerge. Sometimes, the answers would reveal themselves in contemplative moments or while pondering the options and circumstances. In other instances, creating a 'pros and cons' list helped shed light on the different aspects of the decision, enabling a more balanced evaluation. The resolution would arise from a combination of trusting my intuition, deliberate reflection and thoughtful analysis.

The concept of living a life based on intuition is undeniably liberating. It frees us from overthinking, second-guessing and the need for constant, rational justification. That's what we do, we humans. We think we're rational beings but we're emotional beings, imposing rationale over feelings. It's related to our patriarchal and scientific world view, and fits in with the way we are taught at school. It aligns with our sense of time and of living our lives.

By surrendering to our intuition, we tap into a limitless reservoir of guidance and inspiration. It invites us to trust the unseen, embrace uncertainty with a feeling of adventure and live authentically—all while aligning our true desires and values. Living a life guided by intuition doesn't mean abandoning reason or forsaking responsibility. It invites us to harmonize the logical mind with the intuitive heart, creating a synergy that leads to profound personal growth and fulfillment.

My weekend away on the Sunshine Coast became a transformative experience that challenged the conventional decision-making paradigm. We were going to move there, of that, I was sure.

TAKEAWAY

I learnt from this experience that I held a strong faith in my intuition. I could trust myself with one of the most significant decisions of my life. What did you become aware of during this chapter?

CHAPTER 6

DEVELOPING INTUITION

"Intuition is the key to unlocking our inner wisdom and finding clarity amidst the chaos."

—Deepak Chopra

After returning that weekend from Charlotte's house, I kept wondering how it was that I had come to trust my intuition? It had been a process.

After losing Mum when I was 21, I worked with a beautiful Gestalt therapist to help me cope with my grief and make sense of my changed world without my mother. The therapist showed me breathwork as an avenue for personal transformation. It shifted my awareness, fostering change within me. I had such inspiring experiences while participating in these sessions which further confirmed my understanding of myself, my place in the universe and learning to trust in my intuition. Always having been an avid reader, I read books on the subject, attended seminars and workshops to learn from reputable sources; and immersed myself in podcasts. I even consulted friends who had gone through similar experiences (typically, women slightly older than myself), to see what I could learn from them.

My personal growth continued during the years I worked as a herbalist. That was something I loved as it gave me the opportunity to look at the world from an inherently holistic perspective. I experimented with various forms of meditation and spiritual exercises that were not tied to any one religion. This influenced my understanding of the existence of much more in this world than what we can observe with our five senses. During that time, I had sessions with clairvoyants; expanding my insight into the spirit and how to receive intuitive thoughts. These experiences spurred me to trust in my intuition when dealing with people and herbs alike. And so, my confidence grew, knowing that I had the innate wisdom to craft whatever mixture would work best for each client.

Then there were my years of experience as a psychologist! Being formally trained to ask people questions about their feelings and thoughts didn't lead me to use my intuition much. But when I approached my clients as a Gestalt therapist and worked from the space using my intuitive self,

I found a lot more success. That style was more focused on an embodied, experiential approach.

The Gestalt technique calls for being entirely present and receptive to let a 'figure' come to the forefront of one's consciousness. This figure could be anything from an internal or physical sensation, such as a feeling of unease in the throat or chest, that can then be exaggerated or minimized. If done correctly, the result could be a dramatic shift in experience and awareness of something new; and a real change could take place. This, to me, is the practice of using intuition—allowing something to become part of your conscious awareness, both for myself and my client's.

Those twenty or so years had been challenging at times and thank goodness I'd been resilient! I'd lost my dear Mum early on, ran two subsequent businesses and then went through raising four children while navigating a divorce. What I found is if you take the chance to explore yourself, your environment and what lies beyond the physical world, grief can be an enormously effective tool. As painful as it is at the time, you'd be wasting a precious opportunity if you didn't learn from it and grow. The same applies to divorce! It also carries all the components of sorrow. I'd tell my clients, "Don't waste a good divorce!"

And then there was raising my kids! It was life-altering, testing me in every emotion imaginable. The challenges and joys helped me grow, understand more about people and develop my intuitive skills. Like grief and separation did before, this too served as a method of growth. It's all just life! By expanding your understanding through learning and developing your awareness and skills, you can extend into the realm of spirit. As I became more aware of spirit, I tapped into my intuition more deeply and allowed myself to experience so much more of this world.

Through this process, I discovered my inner strength and developed a stronger sense of self. My intuition was essential in helping me make the decision to divorce. Making such a life-changing decision required courage and strength, but I remember at the time that I didn't feel scared to follow my intuition. The anxiety I experienced during the divorce was a reactive product of making such a monumental change in my life. As I have counselled people before, you must confront your fears head on. "Fear knocked on the door; when I opened it, nobody was there" is how I face my fears! You need to take that step forward. So, instead of allowing my fears to dictate my path in life, I chose to meet life with courage.

More and more, I learnt to trust that inner voice, allowing the noise of my rational mind to take a back seat while I followed my heart. Learning happens over the years, facing many of life's challenges and problem-solving as you go. Experiencing positive results from trusting my intuition gave me encouragement to re-establish my self-identity as a single woman and facing future challenges.

Meditation has also had a meaningful impact in my

life. It has helped me find inner stillness, give space for the quietness of mind and allowed my intuition to be gently 'seen' and heard. Through consistent practice, I have developed my meditation skills. You don't have to be a Buddhist monk and spend hours practicing to achieve great results. What you do have to be, however, is consistent in your approach.

My practice involves focusing on breathing for about 10-15 minutes each morning before my mind fills up with the day ahead. I settle into a comfortable chair where no one will disturb me and put on noise-cancelling headphones playing soothing music. Then, I start breathing: inhaling for three counts; pausing; and then exhaling for three counts. My meditation routine is vital for preserving my mental health and makes it easier to tune into the intuitive promptings throughout the day. These appear as ideas coming from outside normal conscious thinking and are accompanied by a particular 'knowing' feeling and a slight, tingly sensation.

I used to tell my clients that controlling their breath through counting techniques can be beneficial to regaining calmness and managing their anxiety. Rather than suggesting they 'meditate' (unless they were comfortable with the term), I used to introduce them to a 'mindfulness breathing exercise'. The exercise would give the anxious person something to focus on; shifting away from the object of their anxiety (and a feeling of being out-of-control).

Focusing on the breath would help create a feeling of control, help reduce anxiety and bring calmness to the mind by creating calmness of the breath.

My journey in developing intuition has taught me that this 'grey' world has no clear right or wrong. Everyone's approach and experience will be distinctively different. Your experiences and approach will differ from mine. Every individual's own intuitive ideas and how they manifest themselves, will be unique.

My path to developing my intuition included my various professional backgrounds, exploring personal interests and learning, dealing with grief and challenges in life, and meditation. An important part of it all was recognizing and trusting the intuitive impulses that arose, distinguishing them from the rational mind's noise. To awaken one's intuition you must embrace stillness, practice mindfulness and cultivate a relationship with your inner voice. Each person's path towards intuition may differ, but the rewards of greater knowledge and direction are priceless. As Eleanor Roosevelt said, *"Nothing has ever been achieved by the person who says, 'It can't be done'."*

TAKEAWAY

- I want to emphasize that each person's intuition is unique. I encourage everyone to do their study and research to help shape their experiences and approaches. Practice sitting still and focus on your breathing. Allow yourself to be open and surrender your disbelief. Just see what happens.

- Have you developed your trust in your ability to 'listen'? First, you need to be able to quieten your mind. If meditation (or if you prefer to call it 'mindfulness practice') could be helpful, then try simply counting your breath: in, two, three, pause, out, two, three, pause. When you notice your mind wandering (and it will), gently come back to focusing on your breathing. I recommend you do this for 10-15 minutes each day.
- Do you feel anxious? If so, persist with this technique of counting your breath to regain calmness. When it's all said and done, your breath is probably the only thing you can consciously control in this world. Most situations fit into the category of something you could influence, not control.

CHAPTER 7

REFLECTION AND DECISION

"In the silence of self-reflection, one finds the courage to soar."
—Donna Goddard

Within a week of returning home from Charlotte's, we had a meeting with Steve, a trusted real estate agent, and had signed the contract to list the house. The process had begun. After he'd left, Matt and I sat on our deck with a bottle of wine and talked over what Steve had been saying about the recent shift in the market and the price we could likely get. The afternoon segued into evening and the bottle was slowly emptied.

In the coming days, I found myself reflecting a lot. I knew this was an important time to understand the factors that had influenced my decision to downsize. Reflection would be my guide, allowing me to unravel the intricacies of my circumstances and gain clarity. Not a complicated process, it was more about taking time to think about what was happening in my life and considering other perspectives occurring at the time. I wanted to do this to help give meaning to my desire to downsize and to see if there were some considerations that weren't purely financial. It had been a psychology technique I had learnt many years ago.

The influence of the planets on our lives has always fascinated me, so astrology was my first reflective port of call. We know that the moon's gravitational pull affects bodies of water and, since we humans are composed primarily of water, it stands to reason that our moods and behaviours also shift due to the changes in its cycle. I'd noticed my pattern over time. During the days leading up to the full moon, I'd get restless and uneasy. This was something paramedics, psychiatric nurses and police officers were also aware of in their respective fields. They'd notice an increase of activity in their jobs on a full moon—a fact which explains why the term 'lunatic' exists.

As I studied the most recent astrological energy, I realized that the celestial alignment was marked by significant energy from Scorpio, which was playing out in both the universe and my life. Humanity had undergone dramatic changes over the last few years and it seemed as if the universe itself was guiding me toward radical change and transformation. This intense energy carried the weight of deep, karmic work, forcing me to confront my fears and unearth uncomfortable patterns. I think the specific energy from Scorpio had directed me towards downsizing although not in an explicit way. Rather than identify the astrological influences then create a plan to downsize accordingly, I had made an intuitive decision to move to the Sunshine Coast and afterwards thought about what was happening on an astrological level. This reflection resulted in me developing a better comprehension of how the universe works.

And then there was the pandemic! Like everyone else, COVID had cast a heavy shadow on our lives, leaving its mark mainly on our financial situation but also on our psyche. The pandemic hit our shores in March 2020 and we experienced several lockdowns over the next two years. Being in a regional area south of Sydney and being able to work from home, we could mostly continue with our lives without too much disruption. We didn't suffer the isolation that many others suffered. One of our businesses, however, had taken a big hit and we closed it for the duration. Thankfully, our other business was somewhat more resilient and, although impacted, managed to continue as a modest revenue stream. That, coupled with our eligibility for government grants to assist with the impact of the pandemic, allowed us to keep our head just above water.

But the collateral damage of the pandemic was clear. Financially, we found ourselves facing significant challenges, prompting the need to reassess our circumstances. We didn't need our accountant or a crystal ball to tell us that downsizing and liquidating our main asset, the family home, was not just a sensible option but a realistic one. So, while the pandemic didn't lead us to downsize, it applied more urgency.

Balancing financial restrictions with emotional attachment to our current home was a crucial factor in our downsizing process and thus, required reflection. We knew that downsizing would impact everyone in our family differently, which was why every member's needs were considered during the decision-making process. Each of my children had reached different stages of independence. Some had already ventured out into the world, carving their own paths, while the two sons still living with us were studying at university, and so were still semi-dependent on us. They were in my mind, however, ready for new beginnings, whether they knew it or not.

The decision to sell would therefore have an immediate impact on some and a distal effect on others. For the girls, who'd grown up in that house, selling the family home meant losing a connection to elements of their childhood, disrupting the lives they had grown accustomed to and severing ties to cherished memories.

When we first began considering to downsize a year or so before, the focus was on looking for properties in neighbouring areas so there would be less impact on the family. When that search yielded no results, there was a pause in our searching until the surprising idea of relocating to another state was put forward by Alex. Subsequently, plenty of individual and collective discussions with the kids were held about the decision and process. Finally, everyone realized that it was time for us to move forward and begin a new stage as a family.

As I pondered family dynamics, I also had to factor in the desire for a smaller and more manageable living space and what that meant for us on a personal and emotional level. Not only was it a financial decision, but also a decision based around being a 'couple' and not a family unit. Matt and I had never been a couple by ourselves. He had an older son and, when we'd met, he'd already experienced life as an 'empty nester'. He'd moved into my home; one with teenage and young adult children. Downsizing and setting up something together also presented itself as an exciting chapter in our lives and one that could take us towards the future.

A lot of this reflection involved my thoughts around Matt and my children. I'm a Cancerian and a mother so it's natural I concern myself with the wellbeing of my children. It was, however, time to think about myself!

I was just in my mid-fifties and physically had moved into a time in my life when nurturing was not my highest priority (yep, call it menopause if you like). The changes I experienced were physical, emotional and spiritual. My body was struggling with a drop in estrogen typical during this life phase and my emotions were also responding. I had disrupted sleep patterns, hot flashes and weight gain. I became invisible in public! My mind was initially vague and wandering everywhere except where I wanted. Eventually I became stronger and my thoughts held more clarity. As I moved through the changes, I gained a greater sense of direction and purpose, and started to have time to consider myself and my needs.

We had one more thing to ponder! Steve had given us a heads-up about the housing market's decline so the emotional journey accompanying the sale of our house was a rollercoaster of expectation and anticipation. We had seen a couple of nearby houses go for what we thought was an incredible price, but Steve had told us we couldn't expect anything near that. At first, we were crestfallen! Selling a house is stressful enough for anyone and when you see what you consider the potential value slipping day by day, the stress levels increase because you perceive a loss. What we had initially anticipated as a lucrative sale at the beginning of the marketing campaign started to shift by about $400,000 less than what we had expected. Through my meditation, however, I resigned myself that this was all part of the plan and that a corresponding lower purchasing power would equate to lower prices when it came time to buy.

During these various factors of influence, I developed a

deeper understanding of my situation and was able to assess what was and was not within my power. My sphere of influence equates to all the elements of my life about which I can make decisions. When I make decisions, they're based on my intuition and all the elements surrounding me, from family dynamics to market forces and the pandemic. I don't have control over any of them, only influence over some. I use the word 'influence' quite deliberately instead of 'control' because if I tried to think about this in terms of control, I would be riddled with anxiety. I realised that control is an illusion, but influence is within my grasp. By acknowledging the elements that shaped my decision, I could navigate the path ahead with a clearer perspective. My reflection encompassed the financial constraints and market forces, and the emotional ties and familial responsibilities that intertwined with my desire to downsize.

Taking a step back to take a broader view opened my 'vision' and that helped me see what else was happening and whether other elements could be considered. It allowed me to see beyond the immediate challenges and setbacks, embracing a broader understanding of the universe's cosmic dance. The connection between astrology, the pandemic, family dynamics and the housing market became more apparent. Clearly, for me, all these threads were intricately woven together, forming a tapestry that depicted the complexities of my life. It was all about where my 'home' was going to be, where was I going to feel at 'home'. And as the saying goes, 'Home is where the heart is.'

In doing this reflective exercise and opening my view, I allowed more into my perspective and, therefore, could appreciate various forces at play. The broader view helped me make more informed decisions. Writing this book has both been cathartic and, hopefully, helpful to others. I've read many books about parenting, about grief and about relationships. There's not a lot about moving from raising a family to being an 'empty nester.' This book also represents a sense of purpose at a stage in life where I now live with a good deal of experience and wisdom.

Of course, there will always be those who haven't had courage to take the steps I have taken. Some will sit in their anxiety and never budge. Others have asked for guidance on our decision-making process, keen to learn from our experiences. The family has adjusted and accepted the decision. I've answered concerns along the way, but I'm not trying to convince anyone. People will make what they will of my life choices. That's not my concern. How people see me is none of my business. The connection between universal forces and downsizing was my response to those forces for my stage in life.

TAKEAWAY

This process of looking at a broader view of my situation helped me appreciate how I was being influenced. I was, in fact, responding to larger forces. Giving yourself some distance from your life can be an excellent exercise.

Ask yourself, "How else can I see this"? Look at what else is happening and why you possibly picked up this book instead of another.

CHAPTER 8

HOW TO TELL THE CHILDREN

"The greatest gifts you can give your children are the roots of responsibility and the wings of independence."

—Denis Waitley

Where my kids were concerned, reflecting about the decision was one thing and another to have a conversation with each. The conversation would require sensitivity, as I had dedicated my life to raising children capable of being successful contributors to society and able to think for themselves. In addition, I needed to let them know that my priorities were changing and that meant focusing on my needs and those of my husband (who was not their father).

This is a difficult call for most mothers as we prioritize

our children's well-being and happiness before our own (what someone once called 'eating the burnt toast'!). I made this choice every day and never thought of putting myself first (my youngest, for example, was seventeen before I even considered playing golf—that was how devoted I was to taking care of them!) Still, I felt that I should listen to my intuition which had never wronged me in the past.

On one hand, I was concerned how this may influence their lives, but I reminded myself that a gentle nudge now and then may also be beneficial for their growth. It's like the swan on the lake, choosing to 'encourage' their young to find a new lake of their own.

My two sons, Harley at twenty-four and Jackson at twenty-six, were pretty capable and independent young men. Our move interstate would mean they were close enough for regular visits and, besides, they were easily contactable by phone. Despite this reassuring thought, the storm inside my head persisted. I knew to calm my concerns, it was necessary to cope with my feelings before I had a conversation with each.

I started imagining that as if directly speaking to each individually (I could also have written down some of my feelings as they occurred). Giving a name and acknowledging my emotions allowed me to accept the emotion, then let it go. From my professional background, I knew that if we don't work through our emotions, it's likely that we will store them within; to the point that they will manifest in some areas physically, such as constipation, indigestion or even gall stones.

My initial concerns and fears were that my kids would feel abandoned. Their father had moved away when they were teenagers and I knew that was how some of the kids felt. Being their mother, the guilt and hesitation about prioritizing my needs and moving on with my life were overwhelming. Guilt was paramount. I was challenging a core value of mine—to be selfless in relation to my children.

This was a similar experience I went through with my divorce which impacted the kids directly. Again, I followed a procedure of recognizing my feelings, permitting them to be present in the moment and then letting them go. It's important to note that this strategy can take hours, days or even months to become effective. During this time, the dominant emotion was my sense of responsibility for so many aspects of each child's life for over thirty years. As they matured, my sense of responsibility reduced accordingly.

I tried to imagine myself in their shoes so I could gain an understanding of what they may have been feeling and how to best include that in the conversation. Additionally, with the youngest at 24, they were mature enough to be treated as individuals more than just as 'my kids'.

Of primary importance, I had to make sure that they understood that my decision was based on many factors and had nothing to do with their worth or my love for them. I had a wonderful relationship with them built on a solid foundation of compassion and understanding. Consequently, I simply explained that the move was something I needed to do at this stage in my life. There was no need for me to convince them of my love or their worth.

When my kids and I talked about downsizing, I always spoke truthfully and calmly without overcomplicating the conversation. My words were spoken from the heart. I knew they would understand and, while they might have their concerns and questions, I was ready to reply to them.

As we discussed the practical aspects of downsizing, such as living arrangements or financial changes, I offered logic and reason toward the steps each would need to take to secure a place to live. I helped with getting both boys set up in their houses. It wasn't just one conversation. It became a practically oriented, joint effort in getting them set.

The conversation wasn't without its hiccups. At first, Emma offered some resistance. I handled it by listening attentively to her concerns and letting her speak her mind. I also provided another perspective, helping her understand the change from my point of view. I emphasized the reality that she could still visit her friends in the area whenever she chose, independently from myself.

For all of them, highlighting the importance of staying close even after I moved was unneeded, since it had been my plan all along to stay in contact and visit regularly. They knew that nothing was going to change in our lives apart from the address.

What made me happy was the fact that I not only told them about my decision, but also incorporated them in the decision-making process. When I spoke with Jackson, he'd said that I didn't need to worry, that they would be alright. That allowed me to set aside some of the guilt and responsibility I'd been carrying.

In discussing the downsizing decision, I made sure to highlight the potential positive aspects and opportunities that could arise from the change. I focused on the chance for my kids to be fully independent and responsible for themselves, emphasizing their growth and development through this experience. I also offered Harley the opportunity to move with me interstate; an offer he chose to decline.

We had to ensure that the physical separation wouldn't become a hindrance to our special family bond. So, they agreed to travel for Christmas and enjoy a holiday with us (not just one day). On my end, I committed to personally visiting them regularly and spending quality time with each.

From the conversation with them about downsizing, I gained an unexpected lesson—that I was ready to let go of my responsibilities as a mother. I wasn't aware of this at the time; it occurred to me a year after the move.

After the initial conversation, I wanted to ensure that

they felt heard and understood. Until the actual move, therefore, I would keep in touch through regular telephone chats and, for the boys at home, checking in with them over dinner and casual opportunities.

Reflecting on my approach to talking about downsizing, I believe that being compassionate and thoughtful helped ease their transition (and thus mine). By expressing love and positivity and providing a helping hand, I managed to foster an atmosphere of understanding. Downsizing was hard and included many obstacles besides the emotional implications of leaving our home that held so many special memories. We may have faced challenges during this shift in our lives, however, it also brought us closer together.

TAKEAWAY

My advice to parents in a similar situation who don't know how to communicate with their children: keep it honest, simple and straightforward. Talk to your kids with compassion as transitioning might be intimidating for them, especially when the stability in their home is being challenged. Don't try and make it into anything else; just share your plans and let them know that they can handle the alteration. Remember to listen more than you speak.

CHAPTER 9

PUTTING THE HOUSE ON THE MARKET

*Life isn't about waiting for the storm to pass –
it's about learning to dance in the rain.*

—Author unknown

And then it rained and rained and rained! After signing the contract with Steve, we were given a week to prepare the house to be photographed and videoed for the marketing campaign. This was the easy part! We could hide any unnecessary clutter away, take a photo, move stuff out of that room, take a photo and so on. Matt also cleaned up the yard and gardens, and did runs to the tip. By the end of the week, it was looking schmick.

We were familiar enough with the process to understand that a neat, orderly and uncluttered house was critical for potential buyers to see themselves living there. Steve's photographer/videographer did a fantastic job. Before long, the house was listed, open houses were scheduled and an auction date was set. And then? Well, that's when the actual work started.

It represented a confronting reality! Presenting the house in its best light prompted us to start thinking about downsizing possessions and what items we needed to let go. I felt it an important exercise. I'd moved several times before and found it easy to reduce belongings with each move. Matt, on the other hand, was a bit of a Bowerbird and found it a lot harder to let go of things. In the end, he admitted he kept a lot more than necessary. Eventually, we discarded more when we moved into our new home.

For most people, it's tough to give up sentimental objects. Each family member had their own emotional process of dealing with the items that held memories. We had moments of nostalgia and attachment, but also took our time to consider the importance of each item. Did it still have a purpose in our lives? Did it evoke strong emotions? A major challenge in this process was needing to keep the house from looking cluttered during the open days, so stockpiling boxes with what we wanted to keep was also a challenge.

The kids also needed to pitch in with the presentation

of the house and be supportive. We all agreed that their main responsibility was maintaining their respective room and keeping clutter out of sight (I admit I had to help a bit with that as their sense of clutter and mine were vastly different). Additionally, they needed to be out of the house at inspection times to allow potential buyers to explore freely without distractions.

And speaking of rooms, I also had to find the boys somewhere nearby to rent while they completed uni. Addressing their anxieties about all that became my main priority. Jackson, his partner Anna, Harley and I discussed the most suitable types of properties and locations that would be convenient for their part-time work and uni commitments. That narrowed down the search somewhat and was a good start. During these discussions, the idea was put forward that they were all going to rent somewhere together, but the option was left open for Jackson and Anna to have their place, and Harley to perhaps consider a share house, or at least finding something and then finding a flatmate.

A friend I played golf with was a Letting Agent so I chatted with her to see if she could help either directly or even with advice. And so, the search began! Finding somewhere suitable was not easy especially as Harley had a cat and so many places didn't accept pets (it seemed that the recent experience with the pandemic and lockdowns hadn't filtered down to landlords allowing pets). That was another challenge to face! The search continued for several weeks. Meanwhile, our first open house was due to kick off and we still weren't completely ready.

The need to showcase the house while ensuring our family's privacy and comfort during the selling period was a balancing act. As part of the decluttering process, we also had to remove our personal items, like family photos, from display. We looked on the web at images of houses being listed and they all looked devoid of any personal touches apart from a generic style that looked like the same interior decorator had been used for all. That, apparently, was the 'go' and would allow potential buyers to imagine their own style and belongings in the space. So, the house looked spotless, almost like a blank canvas, ready for the next artist.

And speaking of a blank canvas, just keeping the house spotless with five people still living in it was pretty demanding. Everyday household chores—dishes, laundry and dust—had to be constantly managed to maintain the pristine condition of the house while still living there. Everything needed to be perfect and, frankly, that's not how people normally live and certainly not how my family rolled! I will say, however, that having the open house schedule provided us with a structure over our weekly routine. The Wednesday and Saturday were to start the campaign and then each Saturday would become the routine. I managed these stresses by cleaning and tidying inside and Matt concentrated on getting the outside, especially the back entertaining area, looking inviting (he even lit the fire in the fire pit and had the garden lights on for the first open house).

That first Wednesday came quicker than expected and the house was ready. Steve arrived and put down some brochures and we left him to his devices. We were nervously excited. Our house was on show. Would someone see the potential? Could they see themselves living there? Would they make an offer?

After an agreed hour away, we came back and saw Steve saying goodbye to the last couple. He turned to us and smiled. Half a dozen or so had inspected the house and, while there had been no offers, a few had been interested. The price that some of them had mentioned, however, appeared to be a stumbling block and well beneath what we were wanting. He told us that it was "early days" and, as it was Wednesday, to wait for the coming Saturday when they were expecting more people and interest. On top of that, Saturday was to be a beautiful, sunny day.

We tried to keep the house spotless during those ensuing days, but early Saturday morning saw us jump once again into our respective tasks. The floor needed mopping, the bedrooms needed to be made-up, the grass needed cutting and leaves blown, the fire pit emptied and restacked with kindling… Before we knew it, Steve was at the door and, once again, it was 'showtime'.

After lighting some scented candles and having a last check that everything was in order, we took ourselves (and pets) down the road for a coffee and brunch (having not wanted to make breakfast at the house for fear of leaving a breakfast smell and creating unnecessary mess). Both boys and Anna had to go to work so that was easy for them not to be there.

Again, we returned after the agreed time and Steve was smiling. In his opinion, they'd had a fantastic turnout. Yes, there had been some neighbours stickybeaking, he said, and there were the usual 'tyre-kickers' as he called them, but there had been a couple who had taken contracts. The downside was that, again, a lower price seemed to be on the cards. Despite that, our first week was, in his words, 'a great success' and 'promising'. And then it rained and rained and rained!

The heavy rain we experienced during the rest of the selling period presented a number of difficulties. We adapted by keeping extra mats at the entrance and back door to prevent wet footprints from marring the clean house. But we couldn't brighten up the outdoor entertainment area which just looked sodden and hardly inviting. Despite the weather challenges, we tried to continue presenting the house in its best light.

Steve, as agents do, spun the story to those inspecting that they could see how well the house held up under extreme conditions. It provided a testament to the house's resilience and gave potential buyers confidence that the property was well-maintained and there were no leaks. He even told us that more people come to inspections on rainy days and that the rain was working in our favour. I wasn't necessarily convinced but trusted my intuition that all this—the weather, the process—was happening for a reason.

We were lucky when it came to choosing Steve. Matt had a life-long friend who'd been in real estate his entire working life and, although he lived up in Sydney, gave us a referral to a local agent he trusted. That was Steve. Finding an agent with integrity to handle what is arguably the biggest financial decision of one's life, can otherwise be daunting. If you have connections with a trusted networking group, you may have a better chance to connect with the right person. Checking their individual portfolio of recent sales and looking out for reviews or referrals from previous clients could also give an idea of how good they might be. In my case, it did help that I had a good feeling about the recommendation from Matt's friend and that's why we signed up so quickly. Had my intuition not given me that insight, recommendation or not, I would have looked elsewhere.

After each open day, Steve provided us with feedback regarding who appeared interested, the level of seriousness of potential buyers and the various price points being discussed. It became evident that getting our desired price was not going to happen. Matt once again contacted his friend in Sydney to determine where the overall market stood and what we should do next. We learnt that property prices had spiked hugely months prior but were now starting to decline—the market was definitely softening and the landslide was imminent.

We discussed the initial asking price for our house and the comments from prospective purchasers, at which point Matt's friend gave him the sage advice to "grab the money and run". His opinion was that property prices were going to drop substantially and wouldn't come close to our desired amount for several years. We discussed two options: continue with the campaign and lower our expectations or take the house off the market and hunker down until more attractive values resurfaced.

It was then I realised there was another factor to consider. What was the market doing up in Queensland where we were thinking of buying? Was it still inflated or was it also slowing down. Again, Matt's friend, being well connected in the industry, called in some favours and we got the report that the Sunshine Coast market was still quite buoyant. Many people, just like we were thinking about doing, had been downsizing from around Sydney and Melbourne and buying up there. That was keeping prices relatively high. Eventually, he told us, the market up there would turn—it was all just a matter of time. Our concern, therefore, was that our price appeared to be dropping but where we wanted to buy was remaining high.

One evening and with all that information at hand, Matt, being a visual sort of person and one favouring logical solutions, grabbed a decent bottle of shiraz he'd been saving, a pen and paper, and we sat down to discuss the various scenarios. He wrote down our pros and cons for either selling now or postponing until later, plus financial figures to match. He then asked me what I thought before quickly rephrasing that to: "More importantly, what do you feel?" I looked at Matt's scribbled figures on the page and, for a moment, they all seemed to blur. All I knew was that my intuition was still telling me to go for it. And that's all it took. We clinked our glasses together to confirm our mutual agreement to continue. We were back on track and focused on taking each open house as it came.

Looking back, I can see that maintaining motivation and optimism throughout the downsizing process required support from every member of the family. Matt and I leaned on one another, engaging in open and frequent conversations to reassure and uplift each other. Sometimes, having a different perspective from a loved one can shed light on the situation and provide much-needed motivation. Communicating with our children about the importance of supporting our plans and finding rental accommodation nearby involved open and honest discussions. We emphasized the significance of this chapter in our lives and how their support would contribute to a successful transition. Their response was positive, with Harley especially appreciating the help and Jackson also having Anna's support for their discussions and decision-making.

In the end, the experience of preparing and presenting our house to potential buyers had unexpected positive outcomes and valuable lessons. We learnt more about ourselves, particularly in terms of letting go of expectations and the value we attach to material possessions. The process also strengthened our relationship as we discovered how we dealt with stress and found ways to support one another. This was an important time.

TAKEAWAY

Looking back, the advice and insights I would offer to anyone preparing to put their house on the market and embark on the downsizing journey are:

- Do your homework. Determine how much your home is worth without spending any money. Agents offering to help you sell your property will also suggest what you should renovate or leave unchanged. In our scenario, agents said it wasn't worthwhile doing anything with the kitchen and bathroom

as there wouldn't be a return on investment and it would be better to let the owner decide themselves regarding the design.
- If in doubt, throw it out. Decluttering and getting rid of unnecessary possessions are important and should be done regularly. I have a friend who says that if something comes into the house, something should go out. I am still working on Matt to adopt this approach.
- Get trusted advice. Ensure you have someone you trust and who is qualified or informed to give you advice. There are always plenty of neighbours, acquaintances and even relatives who'll think they know best and will advise you. Make sure you are listening to the right sort of advice.
- Have support. It's hard enough to handle all this stress when you have a partner to help you alleviate some of it. If no one seems available, take people up on their genuine offers of help because it's challenging to do this alone. I have a good friend who would love to move interstate to be with some of her children and grandchildren, but she is struggling with tackling the project on her own. It can be done. You will just need to seek support.
- Communicate. Make sure that everyone who could be affected by such a move knows how you feel, what worries you have and what concerns you may

have about the transfer. Include your kids in decisions and explain why things are happening. Most importantly, don't justify your 'why'. You are not responsible for other people's reactions and this is something, as a parent, which is crucial as you move into another stage of your life.

CHAPTER 10

WAITING FOR THE HAMMER TO FALL

"The house you looked at today and wanted to think about until tomorrow may be the same house someone looked at yesterday and will buy today."

–Koki Adasi, Koki & Associates, Inc.

A uction day finally came. The open inspection days had produced a small, mixed bag of potential buyers. We already knew that the market had started to slide and Steve again advised us not to expect what we had first thought our house was worth at the start of the process six weeks prior. Matt and I were both a little disappointed, especially after all the hard work put into preparing the house for each of the open days and all that rain. We knew, however, that one never knows how an auction could go. If two buyers wanted it enough, they could push up the price. We just had to wait and see.

And the rain decided to come back for the auction! The original plan was to have it outside in our lovely entertaining area but, with the rain, it was moved inside. We were advised to stay out of view and so camped out in our garden office to wait for news from the auctioneer and Steve. While we waited nervously, we discussed what least amount we would settle on and how firm we thought we could be on negotiating given that the market had changed from being a seller's to a buyer's. We even discussed whether we should pass the property in if we didn't get our reserve and postpone the auction for another day in the hope more buyers would discover our 'gem' on the South Coast. We had done our sums, knew in our minds what we wanted and so it was in the hands of the auctioneer.

Not long had passed and Steve appeared at the door to give us an update. There were not many bidders! The auction had not started well and was already sitting below our reserve. Steve told us that the auctioneer had put the two main bidders into separate rooms to speak to each individually and try to get them to increase their bids as there had been a bit of a stalemate with each one not willing to go further in the open setting. He dashed back out the door to get back to the action.

I looked at Matt and the emotions started to well. Looking back, I think it was a combination of all the stress and sheer tiredness. We were both exhausted! Matt held my hand in reassurance. Of course, he was asking me to hone my intuition. It was tricky! There was so much going on—emotions were high, there was the pressure to sell, our expectations, our hopes, our dreams—I didn't know if I could feel or sense anything at that point but I knew I had to try. I closed my eyes and calmed myself by controlling my breathing. "It will be alright," I reassured Matt, "it will be okay!"

Steve appeared again. "We have each of them up to the reserve," he said with a smile, "I don't think we will get much more but what are your thoughts and what do you instruct me to do?"

The relief was immense! I looked at Matt as if to say, "I told you so". He smiled knowingly back at me. Matt thanked Steve and asked him to get whatever 'cream' he could and that we were prepared to now accept the best offer and would sell. Steve nodded his understanding and dashed back out into the rain towards the house.

In the end, he and the auctioneer secured another $20,500 from the eventual buyer and the deal was done. Somehow a bottle of champagne appeared (I think from Steve) and we thanked the auctioneer with a toast before he and Steve turned the toast around to us. We had sold our home! Matt and I were thrilled. Tears of relief rolled down my cheeks! The emotional roller coaster of preparing the house, those open days and now the final auction stress, they were all over. Now we could start the next stages in the downsizing process —the final packing, saying goodbye and looking for a home. It was not over yet. For now, however, we drank in the moment and popped another bottle of bubbles.

CHAPTER 11

NAVIGATING THE EMOTIONAL TERRAIN OF DOWNSIZING

"Holding on is believing that there's only a past; letting go is knowing that there's a future."

—Daphne Rose Kingma

As I started the process of assessing what we wanted and didn't want to take to whatever would be our home, I realized two things: that downsizing was all about 'letting go' and, secondly, that it was not as easy as I thought it would be.

Items that held sentimental value, woven with the emotions and memories they carried, were the hardest to let go. Certain books on my shelves, for example, represented key stages of self-discovery and personal growth. They reminded me of my transformative journey years before. There were pieces of art that had been lovingly gifted by talented artist friends. They hung beautifully in our current house, but would they fit as well in the new? Evoking shared experiences, friendship and the beauty of creative spirits, they meant a lot to me. The sheer process of evaluating whether to keep them or not was a weighty process in itself (in case you are wondering, yes, of course, I kept them). At times, I even found myself deliberating over serving ware, like a salad bowl or serving plate, which held the warmth and joy of countless gatherings and shared meals over laughter.

When it came to photos, both Matt and I each had boxes of them. These cherished reminders of precious moments and life's milestones had mostly been digitized for extra safe keeping, but I felt I couldn't discard the originals. They were too precious. Again, just the process of thinking about this, making the decision and allocating space for the boxes was part of the process!

Objects which were representative of my children's growth and development held special significance. There were handmade cards, paintings and Mother's Day presents made in Primary School, odd toys and things picked up on the beach while on holidays—these were much harder for me to part with, probably because, in some way, I was letting go of a period in my life and in my role as a mother.

This is where grief played a major role. My downsizing coincided with moving into a new stage of womanhood (the 'Upgrade' as I would eventually come to know it) and the changes I was experiencing were inevitable. I told myself that it was time to navigate this labyrinth of emotions and embrace the necessary release while also honouring the past that had shaped me. Who knew that in the deliberate dance of downsizing, my every decision would become a tangible reflection of my life journey, where each object held its unique story—of joy, development and emotional growth—all linked together.

As a psychologist, I could fathom that it was grief all on its own. I think it would be fair to say I felt a certain degree of anxiety and that played out as overthinking. Quite a few times, I would lie in bed in the wee hours when I should have been sleeping, just wondering what I was supposed to leave behind! Mostly, however, I would decide at the time, during the sorting process, whether I would be packing a specific item or letting it go. Perhaps a more accurate description would be one of feeling overwhelmed with all the decisions that needed to be made. The actual decision was more straightforward. I managed these feelings by getting into action and shifting the thoughts into behaviours.

It was certainly a stressful time and, interestingly, somewhat liberating to walk away with less baggage. But that feeling of liberation came later, not at the actual time of downsizing. The overall experience with downsizing was one of letting go and the subsequent grief around letting go, a double-edge sword! The emotions encountered were the same as with other forms of grieving. They ranged from denial, anger, bargaining, depression and acceptance. These aren't linear emotions! They can occur in any order and can re-occur at any time, both during and following the downsizing process.

I turned to various strategies and techniques to cope with the overall grieving process I was experiencing. Journaling became an invaluable outlet for expressing my thoughts and emotions. Writing down my reflections in complete sentences or even single words, allowed me to process my feelings and gain clarity. Putting pen to paper had a therapeutic effect, providing a type of release and helping me make sense of the complex emotions I was experiencing.

In addition to that, I made a conscious effort to maintain connections with loved ones and engage in activities that brought me joy. Regular phone calls with friends and family reminded me of my support network and the meaningful relationships that extended beyond material possessions. I also made time for activities like walking, swimming and playing golf—activities that nourished my well-being and provided a semblance of normalcy amidst the downsizing chaos.

Then, during the downsizing process, I also experienced moments of unexpected anger that manifested as tears. A raw and intense emotional response, it sometimes caught me off guard. Additionally, there were instances of frustration, especially when Matt and I held differing opinions on what to keep and let go, and the timing of the process. We had many conversations navigating these emotions and trying to understand each other's perspectives. Then there was sadness; the sadness of leaving behind my past. But I acknowledged it and allowed myself to shed a tear or reflect on the memories associated with certain items and left it at that. At the same time, however, it helped to remind myself of the bigger picture and the opportunity for a fresh start, a lighter burden and a new chapter in my life.

Bargaining with myself became a natural part of the journey. Sometimes I found myself see-sawing between holding on and letting go, grappling with the sentimental value and practicality of each item. I knew that struggling with the sense of loss could send me into a spiral of reflection that could become quite negative. I didn't want to end up being depressed. I decided that the easiest way to deal with these conflicting emotions was to wrap up the said item and pack it in the moving boxes, giving myself time to revisit the decision later. This is how I struck that delicate balance between honouring my attachments and making room for my future.

I also faced moments of denial, though this was much more in relationship to the decision-making process than the entire downsizing project. There were days where I avoided even entertaining the idea of deciding which item to pack and which to let go. Or even which room to tackle next! The house was filled with boxes, so I worked on one room first, and that room became the storage facility for all packed boxes. And when denial reared its head, I wouldn't even enter that room. Thankfully, those days were few and far between and the decision-making process forged ahead.

TAKEAWAY

- Grief comes in many forms. The process is a lot easier if you can understand and name what you are experiencing. But you will still grieve. There's no avoiding it. The grieving process is a natural part of this transition. Just like any form of loss, it takes time and understanding to navigate through the emotions that arise. Allow yourself the space and grace to feel whatever comes up, whether it's sadness, nostalgia or even moments of resistance. Be patient with yourself and trust that the grieving process will give way to a renewed sense of optimism and fulfillment with time.
- Before you start a downsizing journey, understand that it's not just about letting go of physical possessions. It is also about making space for experiences,

relationships and growth. As you make decisions about what to carry forward, visualize the life you want to live in your new home. Think in terms of functionality, simplicity and the items holding deep meaning for you. I realized that the memories and relationships I cherished were not tied to material possessions. They were within me and no matter wherever I go, I will carry them in my heart forever, regardless of the items I keep or discard.

- Let me add that downsizing is an individual journey unique to each of us. Your experience may be different from mine. A lot would depend on your personal circumstances. But I would still say that it is an opportunity to grow.
- Make sure you have a good support network and use self-support techniques such as journaling. Continue to do the things that bring enjoyment and fulfilment to your life instead of putting them on hold. We need to continue life, not have a hiatus from it while we fill boxes.
- By now, I know the importance of self-compassion. If you are in the same situation, understand that your sentiments are valid and normal. I do suggest, however, that it is important to name them. Also, don't be too hard on yourself. Make space and time to grieve, but also give yourself permission to let go. Trust me; it's okay.

CHAPTER 12

TRANSITIONS AND CONNECTIONS - SAYING GOODBYE TO A BELOVED COMMUNITY

We leave something of ourselves behind when we leave a place, we stay there, even though we go away."

—Pascal Mercier, *Night Train to Lisbon*

I knew it was going to be hard saying goodbye to my friends and neighbours. Over the years, I'd developed some beautiful relationships. I would always stop and chat with my neighbours as I walked to the beach for a swim or when taking the dogs for a walk. I believed I was lucky to have these people in my life; they were just so friendly and sociable, and that helped increase my sense of belonging. This was the place I called home. That feeling of community was something special. I could never go into the local supermarket, for example, without bumping into someone I knew and having a chat. Sometimes I'd spend double the time I needed in the shops just to keep in touch. I had realised early on that staying connected with people takes time and effort. Throughout my thirty years in our little 'seaside village', I made sure to put in the energy to cultivate and maintain relationships with those around me.

There were also many dear friendships that had been developed over those years. Many of these had come about because our children had attended the same school and were friends themselves. On many the odd occasion, we'd hold weekend get-togethers sharing simple food and wine. We'd even take turns inviting each other to our respective homes for 'Sunday drinks' while the kids played outside.

Camping holidays together were a hit with both children and adults. Sitting around the campfire under the stars after a full day on the beach; snorkelling, sailing or kayaking; or going for long hikes, were all special (even when it rained). And then there were the skiing holidays and all the fun out on the slopes and back at the lodge playing board games or cards. Looking back, it seemed that the kids were not the only ones who benefitted from the great time growing up; we, as parents, also profited from a strong sense of belonging and support, and the friendships that were forged. We were there for each other as we each faced our life challenges, from divorce to deaths to raising children.

    This had been my home, my neighbourhood, my life. This was the very location where I'd raised the kids, swam in the ocean pool most days of the year and played golf at the local course. I'd been an active member of the community: volunteered at the local school in the canteen and reading to the kids; helped with the local soccer club and transported children to games; I was there at Nippers during the surfing season; an active member of the early morning swimmers club; had organized our street Christmas party each year; and volunteered at the local golf club. These experiences had been part of shaping my identity and building multiple relationships. These connections also became even more evident during the challenging times we faced during the COVID lockdowns. Back then, our world changed not only drastically but also rapidly. The importance of community and sense of belonging had never been more apparent and needed.

    So naturally, acknowledging and saying farewell to such a close-knit community filled me with emotion. I realized that I would probably not see many of these people again, so saying goodbye was going to be difficult. And that's why we organised a farewell party we called 'The Last Hoorah'.

A sentimental and memorable occasion, this gave us an opportunity to gather all our special friends at our home with an atmosphere akin to the many parties we had hosted over the years. There we could reminisce and laugh about funny experiences we'd shared: about the early days of raising young children; spending endless hours at the beach; and all the camping and adventures. And just like we'd done so many times before, out came the guitars and we sang and laughed and sang some more.

As the evening drew to a close, our closest friends remained. In those moments, there was a tinge of sadness amidst laughter and tears. These were people who knew how much they were loved and how significant they were to me. Our coming together was a wonderful chance to say to them individually how much I valued our relationship. Sometimes, words were not needed. Just a warm hug was enough. I gave lots of warm hugs that night.

This was a bittersweet experience. On one hand, I was excited for the adventure that lay before me; while on the other, I felt a tinge of anxiety about the tasks that still lay ahead. There was also a touch of guilt in leaving behind my youngest son, Harley, and melancholy in parting ways with the wonderful friends and neighbours who had become like family. While I held no regrets about our decision to downsize, I couldn't help but feel the weight of grief as I started to say the final goodbyes to my friends and also that chapter of my life.

Once we had completed the move and settled into our home, it took many months for my grief to run its course. Since those days, whenever I would visit the old neighbourhood, a strange mixture of emotions would engulf me. It was mostly a feeling of being in a familiar place and seeing familiar faces, but there was the stark realisation that it was no longer my home. It was a strange mix of belonging and detachment; a reminder of the profound impact a place and its people can have on our lives. I guess I had become a familiar visitor!

TAKEAWAY

- The downsizing journey taught me that allowing ourselves to experience the full range of emotions is important. It's natural to feel sadness, grief and even moments of denial when leaving behind a place we have called home for so long. Acknowledging these emotions, accepting them as an inherent part of the transition and finding healthy ways to navigate through them is crucial for our well-being.
- Reflecting on my experiences, I realize I had built an incredible bond within a community over a long period. I was able to acknowledge how all

those relationships were intertwined to give me belonging and support. Think about the many relationships you have developed over the years and perhaps don't wait to tell those around you that you value your relationship. Throw a party and celebrate friendship.

- In the end, downsizing went beyond simply letting go of physical possessions. A mixed bag of experiences, it required me to navigate the emotional landscape of farewells while also embracing the uncertainties of my life's unfolding chapter. It showed me the value of community and relationships. As I was ready to start this phase of my life, I carried with me a deep appreciation for those cherished moments and these lovely connections. If you are contemplating a similar experience, be prepared to get your compass out and navigate that emotional landscape yourself.

CHAPTER 13

MOVING DAY: EMBRACING A NEW BEGINNING

"The secret to change is to focus all of your energy not on fighting the old, but on building the new."

—Socrates

The weeks leading up to the moving day were filled with excitement, anticipation, grief and the daunting task of boxing up our entire lives. By now, our small, four-bedroom cottage was bursting at the seams with taped-up boxes under the house, in the office and the garden shed. It was not starting to become a reality; it was our reality!

Now that we had an actual moving date, I could

organize and pack to that. Sorting through everything, cleaning and deciding what to pack or discard was quite a challenge. I relied on my old fallback and went for a systematic approach. I tackled one room at a time and started with items we didn't need in our everyday lives. I left the kitchen, bathroom and wardrobes until last. While packing, I kept cleaning the cupboard spaces so I wouldn't have to revisit them later. I quickly realized that a friend's advice to start early was spot-on as packing took longer than I had initially anticipated.

We were moving interstate, more than 11 hours' drive away. It was also clear we had a lot of 'stuff' to move. I searched the internet for options and asked friends for ideas and recommendations. There were so many! I reached out to my brother who had recently moved from the Sunshine Coast to Brisbane and Matt also spoke to his brother who had recently moved from Sydney up the North Coast.

The logistics of moving interstate were different from the mostly local moves I'd undertaken previously. There were several factors I was trying to consider. Firstly, cost of moving was going to be significant. Secondly, while we were going to stay initially at Charlotte's place for the first few days and then stay at Matt's friend's granny flat for two months, we didn't have an address to move to as we hadn't yet bought anything. That meant we would need some form of storage for some months! That posed another issue—we had several treasured plants we intended taking with us, so they would have to come in the car and not go to storage! We also had to plan what essential belongings would be needed in the car that would be useful while we found our home? The car was going to look like the 'Griswold's on vacation'!

I explored the idea of storage pods which you pack yourself and then are picked up and relocated to a chosen destination or stored. The advantage was when you're ready to unpack, they move the pods to your house and take away the empty ones. That sounded like a good option.

We also considered hiring a truck and driving it ourselves—another sensible option at first thought. But then we decided that it would be too stressful and I would be driving the car with the dogs while Matt would drive the truck for 11 to 12 hours. In the end and based on Matt's brother's experience, we decided to bite the cost bullet and hire removalists to do the whole thing. While it would be a lot more expensive, it would be far less stressful and far more efficient, especially as we thought we were going to be approaching the end of our respective tethers at that stage. Matt booked a storage unit up on the Sunshine Coast, gave the removalists the address and scheduled them to load up the truck. They would drive interstate in a vehicle they were skilled at manoeuvring and then unload at the end. That made a lot more sense so became our plan.

Before I knew, schedule or not, the day of the move arrived quicker than I had expected. We'd already said goodbye to two of our kids who'd already moved out, but saying farewell to Harley, Jackson and Anna who'd been living with us, made my heart heavy. My voice cracked as I hugged them goodbye. Emotions ran high and, as the saying goes, there wasn't a 'dry eye in the house'. It was a moment of profound grief. I struggled to say goodbye but knew it was time to embark on the next adventure.

Standing in front of our old empty house, knowing that this chapter of our lives was ending, was a strange feeling. I realized that the house itself was not as important as the memories and people who had made it home—the people who laughed, cried, shared and sometimes argued. People are what makes a house a home, not possessions! Sure, belongings can give a house warmth and character, but only people can give it a soul.

The emptied rooms made me think back to the day I'd moved in. I'd been brimming with excitement and determination to create a home for us. And I had! It had been a wonderful, warm home for all those years—a place where my kids had grown up, where they had invited their friends, where so many precious memories had been forged. I'd achieved all that and many times, it had been with the help of my intuition. I knew I had it in me to make a home out of an empty house and so would do that again, this time somewhere up on the Sunshine Coast. I had nothing to fear. I was ready to create a home for Matt and me, knowing it would always be a welcoming place for our kids and eventually, their kids. The thought reassured me. I felt a warming sensation spread throughout my body as I stood there saying goodbye. I knew we couldn't go backward, only forward.

Matt put the car in gear and we were on our way. With 11 or so hours of driving ahead, we hit the road with a fully laden car, two dogs, our Spotify list of favourite tunes and my intuition reassuring me all would be fine. Both of us were surprised that neither felt tired. I guess the adrenaline of the move had us alert and energized.

The scenery changed gradually as we moved away from familiar, local landscapes. Our dogs, Maggie and Tilly, our faithful partners on our journey, added an element of joy and companionship. Their presence and antics made us happy so were a welcome distraction. Tilly was ten weeks old while Maggie was a more mature one year old. I wondered what they might have thought about the move and whether they would be unsettled by it. Having had dogs over the years, I knew that, as long as their owner is settled and not stressed, the dogs are usually okay as they can sense the energy of the owner. Call that dog intuition but I have found that to be true. Maggie and Tilly seemed calm and happy in the back seats and we gave them enough pit stops for a run and chasing a ball.

Throughout the long drive, Matt and I chatted away keeping each other company. Our hearts were full of excitement for the unknown before us and we channelled these emotions into a positive mindset by embracing the idea of starting fresh, exploring new surroundings and building a home that reflected our current stage of life. We focused on opportunities not barriers.

As we grew closer to arriving at Charlotte's, I started to become emotional. I was excited to see my beautiful daughter and knew she was equally excited to welcome us. The thought filled me with overwhelming love and happiness. I also realised that our long drive had been our transition. Moving day had now come and gone. It'd been an important day in our lives that marked the end of one chapter and the beginning of another. Leaving behind our family, friends and community had certainly been challenging, but my eyes were focused on my future. Knowing that the memories and experiences we would create in our new home would be worth it all. Our home! Wow. How exciting!

And so, with thankful hearts, we arrived. We stepped out of the car and were warmly welcomed by our beaming daughter. Her smile reaffirmed that we had made the right decision.

TAKEAWAY

- Packing and moving logistics can take longer than planned. I recommend, therefore, that you start early. Make lists and work systematically. This is crucial to managing the sometimes-overwhelming task ahead. Give yourself ample time, both for the practical aspects of the move and for processing your emotions.

- Get quotes from moving companies and look at the options for renting small trucks yourself. The Pods were a good option but didn't work for us. Removalists who do it all can be expensive so do your homework. We found one who simply loaded and unloaded the truck but didn't pack the boxes, so we needed to be ready for the day. The risk was that breakages were basically our responsibility.
- Work to the idea that you have more than you realise. Moving companies often quote according to cubic meters and many have software to help you calculate how much you plan to move. Our driver told us on the day that we had about six cubic meters more than what we had estimated. It was not an issue for him as we had rented his whole van, but it was an issue for our planned storage. Consequently, *en route* we called the storage facility and rented more space. In short, plan about 10-15% more than what you think.

- When choosing a removalist, make sure you get a personal referral or testimonial. Ask them for an honest assessment of what went well or didn't. We ended up using the same company Matt's brother had used based on his experience. They proved to be as good as he said but we did hear some horror stories.

CHAPTER 14

EMBRACING TRANSFORMATION WITH COURAGE, INTUITION AND HUMOUR

"If you haven't learnt how to laugh at yourself, then you've been living life too seriously!"

—*Ruby Robinson*

Just over a year has passed since we bought our home on the Sunshine Coast. It all seems so long ago and we are so happy. My intuition was right.

After staying with Charlotte for those first few days,

we moved into Matt's friend's granny flat for two months while they were overseas. Meanwhile, I searched the real estate market and Matt continued working from home and flying backwards and forwards to Sydney for his consulting work on the South Coast.

After about five or six weeks and quite a number of house inspections, we finally found the place we wanted. I had to laugh at the irony because it was much larger than the little cottage we had sold. In fact, just about every house up here on the Sunshine Coast was bigger—they just built everything bigger up here. The amazing thing, however, was that the property we bought was around a million dollars less than what we had sold. Our downsizing goal had been to free up our main asset, the house. We certainly had achieved that.

As I am writing this, we are undertaking renovations. The house we have made our home was not perfect but had such great potential and needed some modifications. After all, we are deck people and this house didn't have the deck space to capture the amazing views out across to the sea. Charlotte and Alex ended up moving in with us on the lower floor to help save for the deposit for the house they eventually bought. And with the renovations, while we want to make the house a little more comfortable and optimize the stunning ocean views, we have plans to create an Airbnb downstairs that can generate a passive income.

Apart from the obvious change of address, our social

life has also changed. Of course, I can't see old friends as often as before, but I still stay in touch and cherish our bond. Some of them have even been up to visit as have each of our kids. Everyone has been so impressed and marvelled at our location and the potential with the house. Recently, we had to go back down to the old neighbourhood for work, so a perfect opportunity to catch up with old friends. We broke bread and drank wine, Matt played guitar with his old mates and we all sang along—it was just like old times and such a hoot.

And new friends? Yes, I know that building friendships will take time and effort, just like I had to do when I started in my old neighbourhood all those years before. I've already joined the local golf club and, although it's a slow process, it's helping me meet people. And, as I walk Maggie and Tilly most mornings along the stunning off-leash beach, I seem to have already become 'a regular' and it's just a matter of time before I get to know people and friendships will develop.

Matt is still flying down every few weeks as he rounds off his business dealings, but otherwise, he can work mostly from home. He's also looking for opportunities up here and we have our plans for the Airbnb as soon as the renovations are finished. And speaking of flying down, Jackson and Anna recently welcomed their first child into the world and I've been going there frequently to visit. And Emma, also living in Sydney, is expecting soon so we are eagerly awaiting the arrival of our second grandson. Nothing can beat the joy of basking in the happiness of becoming a grandparent. Things can't get better than that. We've already been preparing the rooms here for the pending visits and are so looking forward to the company and sure to have a lot of fun.

As I reflect on my experiences and the lessons I learnt while downsizing, I think that recognising and listening to my intuition was key. Identifying and naming other factors (e.g., grief) that can also come into play while navigating challenging life stages, such as moving and saying farewell, is also immensely helpful. We are all on a journey and the path we follow is full of signposts if we take the time to see them. Some may be obscured by what life throws in the way or by our distractions, but if we adopt a broader perspective that acknowledges the power of intuition and universal forces, we will strengthen our wisdom and be able to follow a truer path. This will allow us to see beyond our immediate circumstances and tap into available guidance and support. Walking through life without recognizing the larger universe and its influences is like wearing blinkers that restricts our vision.

I have also learnt that grief is an inevitable part of everyone's life journey. No one can avoid experiencing that feeling of loss and heartache at some point. I understand first-hand that grief can take various forms throughout life and it's therefore essential to recognize and honour its presence. For instance, I lost my mother at the young age of 21. My grief was overwhelming. In my late 20s, however, I decided that it was time to work on processing that grief. I knew that if I continued to focus on my experience of loss, I would continue to feel the burden of grief. I deliberately chose to see that experience from a different perspective and looked for something positive to emerge. I would try to remember funny memories I had of my mother, recalling the times, for example, when we had giggled together. This shift in my thoughts and feelings made my grief feel lighter and I could finally find positivity amidst the pain.

All feelings are valid and normal! We don't have to run away from them. Instead, we can name what we feel and allow ourselves to experience them without resistance. Being aware of your emotions is the first step. I recall one of my teachers drumming into our group, "Awareness leads to change". He also used to say that it's a bit like driving a car too quickly around a sharp bend in the road. If you try to steer away from the bend it will be a real struggle and you may not make the turn. But if you lean into the bend, steering a little toward the edge, you can regain control of the car and then steer it through the turn! Because avoiding our emotions only adds to our struggle, I have learnt to acknowledge and accept every emotion as it arises, 'leaning' into the emotion. I have also learnt that seeing situations in a different perspective helps tremendously.

There's nothing quite so refreshing as having a good

laugh and I actively seek out humour in my everyday life, looking for the funny side in any given situation. It's no surprise that I applied the same principle to this entire downsizing process, searching for the humour in our experiences of change and transition. Laughing at ourselves and finding the funny side lightens the burden and helps us navigate challenging circumstances. It's not about making fun of the challenges but looking at them with a light-hearted perspective. When faced with a difficult or unusual situation, by being open and asking ourselves the question, "How else can I see this?" we can often see a different point of view and even the humour within. After all, if you haven't learnt how to laugh at yourself, then you've been living life too seriously.

Maintaining a positive mindset and resilience throughout life's ups and downs is a continuous practice. I prioritize not taking myself too seriously and finding humour in every opportunity helps me stay grounded and optimistic. Laughter has been my remedy. Additionally, my resilience was born and nurtured through my childhood experiences. My parents taught me not to dwell on minor accidents or injuries, but to see them as learning opportunities. It might have been tough at times, but this approach has definitely helped me build my coping skills and a positive mindset.

My sense of identity has been transformed as I move into another life stage. This process has cemented my perception of myself as a woman who seeks adventure and lives life with courage, (even though some people's behaviours can still frighten me). Moreover, I have fully embraced my identity as an intuitive being, trusting my inner guidance wholeheartedly.

Thorough research and diligent homework also played a vital role in my overall success and preparedness during the moving process. By gathering information and educating ourselves, I learnt more about downsizing and that also guided me on making the right decisions. Whether it's selling a home, downsizing checklists or exploring different moving options, if you take time to do your research, you can reduce the fear of the unknown and thus eliminate a huge amount of stress. I have always believed in the power of informed choices leading to successful results. Doing your research and balancing that with trusted, first-hand experience will go a long way to having a smooth process.

But it is all up to you and, ultimately, trusting your decision-making process is essential when faced with important life choices. So here is another tip: whenever I faced major life decisions and would feel uncertain or overwhelmed, I wrote down my options and a list of pros and cons. It sounds simple but, in that way, I took them from circling around and around in my head and creating the potential for confusion or anxiety. By putting them on paper, I gained clarity for the decisions at hand. I found that the pure act of making a decision helped me move forward and that in itself increased my self-confidence.

Whatever your circumstances, I hope that you can apply the overall themes and lessons from my experiences to your life, so they may assist your own transformation. Although the specific life challenges may differ, the underlying lessons and techniques remain relevant. Navigate your challenges by pausing and shifting perspectives. Find humour in the situation and embrace a reflective process. These lessons can enlighten your understanding of the grieving process and encourage you not to take yourself too seriously. By expanding your awareness of yourself and the universe, you can approach your challenges differently and make decisions with a broader and clearer view. You can utilize journaling as a tool, for example, and connect with your intuition through meditation, deepening your self-awareness and making decisions with greater clarity and confidence.

After going through my personal journey, I hope you take away the lesson that life challenges are universal and part of the transformative journey of being human. You can see each experience as it presents itself as a challenge or problem to solve and as an opportunity for learning and growth. By allowing yourself to feel and process emotions, and by showing kindness and compassion to yourself, its so much easier to navigate what life throws up with grace and resilience.

All the best for your downsizing journey.